DESERT ANIMAL ADAPTATIONS

by Julie Murphy

Content Consultant
Jackie Gai, DVM
Zoo and Exotic Animal Consultation

CAPSTONE PRESS
a capstone imprint

A+ Books are published by Capstone Press,
1710 Roe Crest Drive, North Mankato, Minnesota 56003.
www.capstonepub.com

Copyright © 2012 by Capstone Press, a Capstone imprint.
All rights reserved.
No part of this publication may be reproduced in whole or in part, or stored in a retrieval system,
or transmitted in any form or by any means, electronic, mechanical, photocopying, recording,
or otherwise, without written permission of the publisher.
For information regarding permission, write to Capstone Press,
1710 Roe Crest Drive, North Mankato, Minnesota 56003.

Library of Congress Cataloging-in-Publication Data
Murphy, Julie, 1965–
  Desert animal adaptations / By Julie Murphy.
    p. cm.—(A+ books amazing animal adaptations)
  Includes bibliographical references and index.
  Summary: "Simple text and photographs describe desert animal adaptations"—Provided by publisher.
  ISBN 978-1-4296-6030-3 (library binding) — ISBN 978-1-4296-7025-8 (pbk.)
  1. Desert animals—Adaptation—Juvenile literature. I. Title. II. Series.
  QL116.M87 2012
  591.754—dc22   2011004818

Credits
Jeni Wittrock, editor; Matt Bruning and Gene Bentdahl, designers; Wanda Winch, media
    researcher; Eric Manske, production specialist

Photo Credits
123RF: Peter Kirschner, 6–7; Alamy: Bruce Coleman Inc./Marvin W. Larson, 18; Alexander Dudley: 20–21; Ardea.com: D. Parer & E. Parer-Cook, 23; DigitalVision: 12–13; Getty Images: Joe McDonald, 8, Theo Allofs, 19; iStockphoto: g01xm, 26–27; James P. Rowan: 24–25; Minden Pictures: Larry Minden, 16, Michael & Patricia Fogden, 22, Mike Gillam, 9, Xi Zhinong, 14–15; Nature Picture Library: Martin Gabriel, 10–11; Shutterstock: Aleksandra Grzeganek, Cover, EcoPrint, 1, file404, Design Element, Jens Peermann, 17, Pavelk, Design Element, Raisa Kana, 28, Vladimir Medvedev, 4–5

Note to Parents, Teachers, and Librarians
The Amazing Animal Adaptations series uses full color photographs and a nonfiction format to introduce the concept of animal adaptations. *Desert Animal Adaptions* is designed to be read aloud to a pre-reader or to be read independently by an early reader. Photographs help listeners and early readers understand the text and concepts discussed. The book encourages further learning by including the following sections: Table of Contents, Glossary, Read More, Internet Sites, and Index. Early readers may need assistance using these features.

TABLE OF CONTENTS

About Desert Animals 4

Body Parts 6

Body Coverings 14

Behavior 18

Glossary 30

Read More 31

Internet Sites 31

Index 32

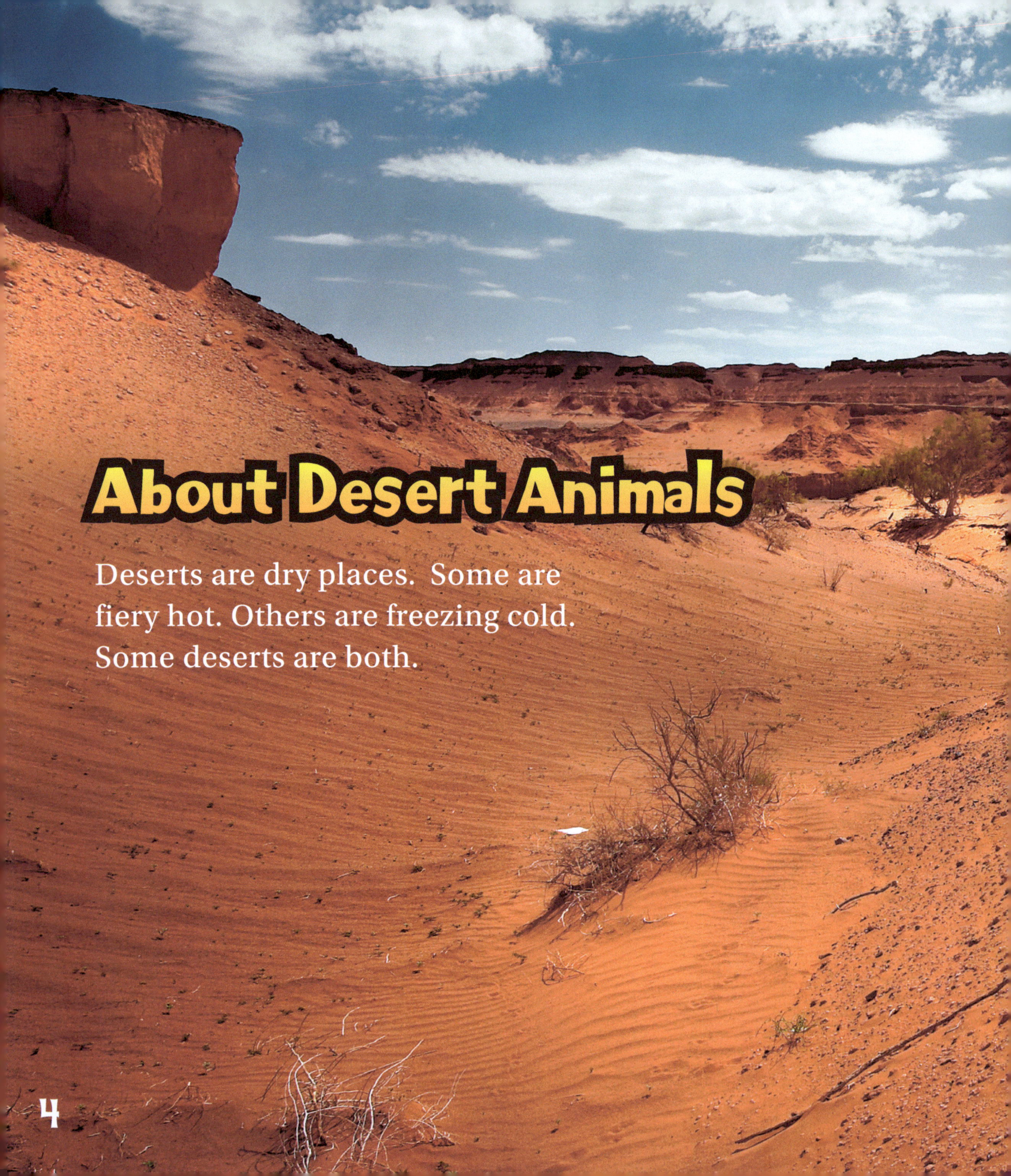

About Desert Animals

Deserts are dry places. Some are fiery hot. Others are freezing cold. Some deserts are both.

Desert animals have special ways of finding food, water, and shelter. These ways are called "adaptations."

Body Parts

Could you keep your cool in a hot desert? The fennec fox does. Jumbo-sized ears release body heat into the air.

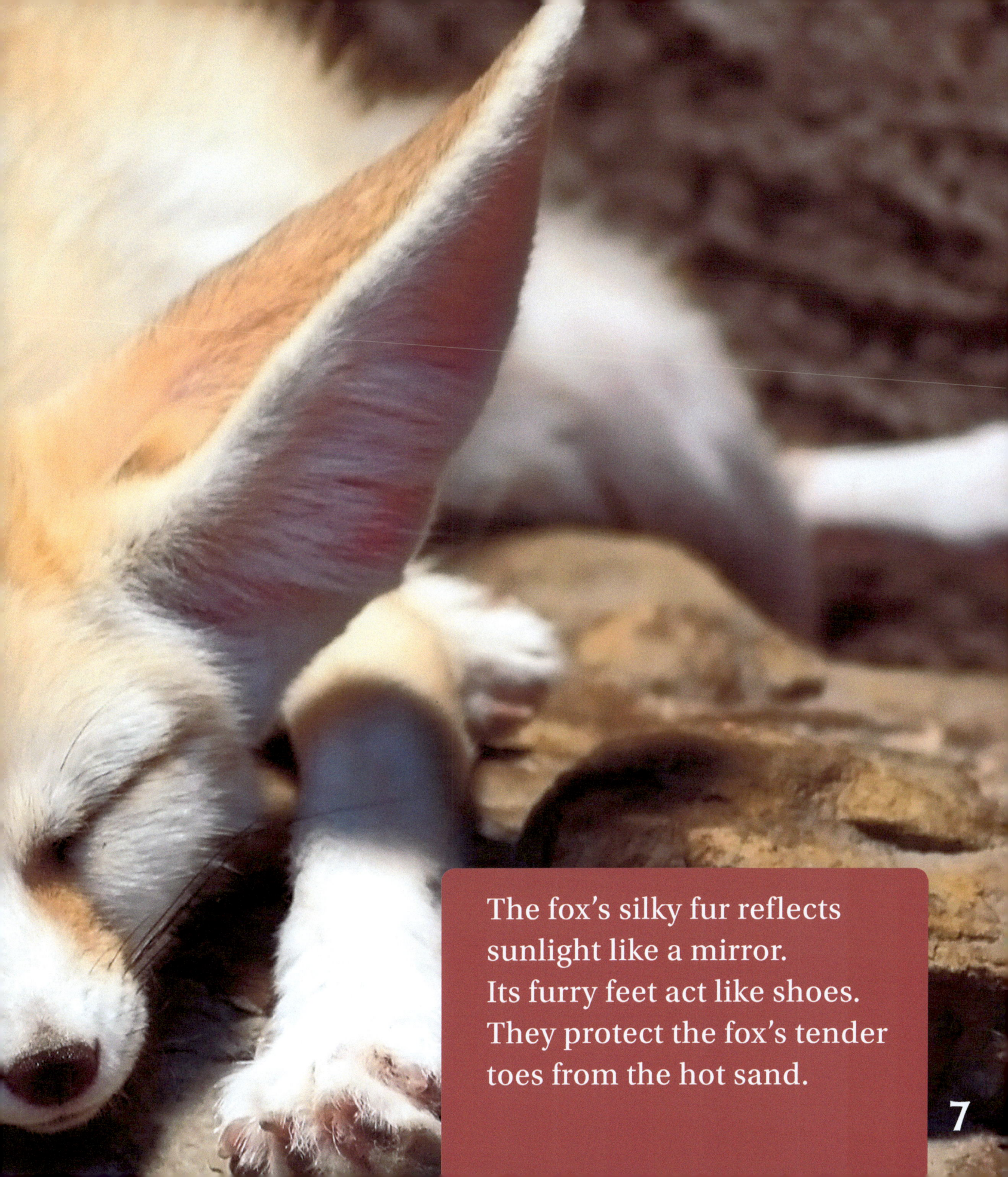

The fox's silky fur reflects sunlight like a mirror. Its furry feet act like shoes. They protect the fox's tender toes from the hot sand.

Kangaroo rats avoid the desert heat a different way. These rats are nocturnal. Their huge eyes see well, even when it gets dark.

Marsupial moles don't need eyes at all! They live in cool, dark tunnels beneath the desert. Scooplike hands are terrific for digging and gripping prey.

Why wear snowshoes in the desert? The web-footed gecko zips across the hot sand without sinking. Wide feet make digging super easy too.

What do camels keep in their humps? Fat! Stored fat allows camels to live several months without eating. How's that for a neat desert trick?

Camels also have double rows of eyelashes and nostrils that close. This keeps sand and dust out of a camel's eyes and nose.

Body Coverings

In very cold deserts, some animals wear two fur coats to stay warm. This yak's long, shaggy hair nearly touches the ground. It is the yak's jacket.

And the soft, warm hair underneath is its woolly underwear!

In hot deserts, thick, scaly skin protects tortoises from the sun. Tortoises store water in their bodies and rarely drink or pee.

Many desert tarantulas are lighter than tropical tarantulas. Dark colors hold in heat. A light-colored body keeps the spider cool.

Behavior

Elf owls nest inside big cactuses. A cactus is cool, shady, and safe from predators.

How does a desert frog keep from drying out? Spencer's burrowing frogs live underground. They only come to the surface to mate after rare heavy rains.

Goanna moms have a clever way to keep their eggs safe in the desert. The lizard digs a hole in a termite mound. She lays her eggs inside.

Termites patch the hole after she leaves. Inside the mound, her eggs stay cool and protected. At hatching time, mom returns to free her babies.

There are many ways desert animals beat the heat. A wheeling spider rolls and bounces along the sand's hot surface.

A pebble-mound mouse builds a pile of stones over its burrow. The stones keep out hot air. The burrow stays cool and cozy all year round.

Thirsty? There is water in the desert, if you know where to look. This white-winged dove sips from a saguaro cactus. Its fruit has juicy nectar.

25

Early in the morning, the thorny devil rubs itself on grass. Dew drops fall onto the lizard's spines and roll into its mouth.

This chart shows desert adaptations mentioned in this book. Can you remember each animal's adaption?

Animal	Behavior	Body Covering	Body Parts
camel			●
desert tarantula		●	
desert tortoise		●	
elf owl	●		
fennec fox			●
goanna	●		

Animal	Behavior	Body Covering	Body Parts
kangaroo rat			●
marsupial mole			●
pebble-mound mouse	●		
Spencer's burrowing frog	●		
thorny devil	●		
web-footed gecko			●
wheeling spider	●		
white-winged dove	●		
yak		●	

Glossary

adaptation—a change a living thing goes through to better fit in with its environment

burrow—a tunnel or hole in the ground made or used by an animal; burrow also means to dig in the ground

dew—small water drops that collect overnight on outside surfaces, such as plant leaves

hatch—to break out of an egg

mate—to produce young

nectar—a mix of juice and pulp

predator—an animal that hunts other animals for food

spine—a sharp, pointed growth

Read More

Gordon, Sharon. *Desert Animals*. Animals in the Wild. New York: Marshall Cavendish Benchmark, 2009.

Kalman, Bobbie. *Baby Animals in Desert Habitats*. The Habitats of Baby Animals. New York: Crabtree Pub., 2011.

Rustad, Martha E. H. *Animal Camouflage in the Desert*. Hidden in Nature. Mankato, Minn.: Capstone Press, 2010.

Internet Sites

FactHound offers a safe, fun way to find Internet sites related to this book. All of the sites on FactHound have been researched by our staff.

Here's all you do:

Visit *www.facthound.com*

Type in this code: 9781429660303

Check out projects, games and lots more at
www.capstonekids.com

Index

burrows, 23
camels, 12–13
coats, 14
desert tarantulas, 17
desert tortoises, 16
drinking, 16, 24, 27
ears, 6
eggs, 20–21
elf owls, 18
eyelashes, 13
eyes, 8, 9, 13
fat, 12
feet, 7, 10
fennec foxes, 6–7
fur, 7, 14
goannas, 20–21
kangaroo rats, 8

marsupial moles, 9
nests, 18, 20
noses, 13
pebble-mound mice, 23
peeing, 16
skin, 16
Spencer's burrowing frogs, 19
termites, 20–21
thorny devils, 27
web-footed geckos, 10
wheeling spiders, 22
white-winged doves, 24
yaks, 14